Sermon on the Mountain the Beatitudes for Children

Matthew 5:3-12,   Luke 6:20-23

Written by Carol Gonsalves
Illustrated by Erin Leigh

ARCH Books

Copyright © 1981 CONCORDIA PUBLISHING HOUSE,
ST. LOUIS, MISSOURI
MANUFACTURED IN THE UNITED STATES OF AMERICA
ALL RIGHTS RESERVED
ISBN 0-570-06149-0

Matthew 5:3-12

Jesse and Anna were twins, you see,
Who lived by the shores of Lake Galilee.

Both the children were peaceful and mild.
They never caused trouble, or ran about wild.

They helped their parents as best they could,
Sweeping the house and gathering wood.

But one day Anna was feeling sad,
And Jesse seemed to be just plain mad!

"I know," said Anna,
    "let's go into town,
Visit the market
    and look all around.

"We might find something
    fun to do—
Something exciting,
    Something new!"

3

Jesse agreed, and off they went
In search of adventure, a grand event.

The marketplace
        was busy and bustling.
Men and women
        were shoving
        and tussling.

They met old Simon,
    a very good scribe,
Who'd never, ever taken a bribe.

6

The children sat and talked to him,
Because he seemed so sad to them.

"O Simon, Simon, why are you sad?
Has something happened very bad?"

"Look, my friends, what do you see?
Sadness and hatred and poverty.

"See old Basil, ragged and torn.
He begs for help, but gets only scorn.

"Hear the widow give a soft moan.
How sad she is; she's all alone.

"Two men there fussing with all their might.
Look! Nobody tries to stop the fight.

"A Roman soldier
    with helmet and sword.
He pays no attention;
    he's really bored.

"The proud young scribes with boastful eyes.
They wear an outward, false disguise."

Jesse frowned, and Anna cried.
"Is no one happy?" the children sighed.

Just then a young man ran into town,
Excited, he shouted and called all around.

"Jesus will speak on the hillside today.
He's God's own Son; His words are the Way.

"So tell all the sick, the poor, and the blind.
Bring everyone here that you can find."

"Who is this Jesus?" asked Anna, amazed.
"They say He's
        God's Son,"
        said Jesse,
        still dazed.

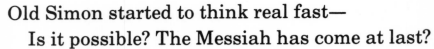

Old Simon started to think real fast—
   Is it possible? The Messiah has come at last?

   "Then to the mountain we must go!"
      They joined the crowd
         that was moving slow.

They saw old Basil, sick and frail.
They saw the widow, old and pale.

They saw the folk from the marketplace.
Not one single smile was on their face.

The two fussy men; the young scribes with their pen;
Even the Roman soon joined in.

It was quite a crowd on the hill that day.
It was hot and dry, no room to play.

One man grumbled, "I can't wait all day
Just to hear what this Jesus has to say!"

"Be quiet, you big mouth," someone shouted.
"Be patient, like me," another man touted.

Simon the scribe sat with scroll and pen.
And Anna and Jesse sat beside him.

The crowd still buzzed like a hive of bees,
When out came Jesus from among the trees.
And with Him came a cooling breeze,
That put the noisy crowd at ease.

Jesus began:

"There is a glorious kingdom
For those who do believe.
I am sent by God above;
My message to you is one of love.

"Blessings are in store for you
Who live the life
     God wants you to."

He spoke as though He knew the heart
Of every person from the start.

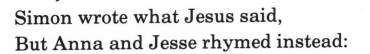

Simon wrote what Jesus said,
But Anna and Jesse rhymed instead:

Be happy—
If your spirit's low,
   no need to grieve
The kingdom of God
   you will receive.

Be happy—
If you weep and are upset
I shall make you soon forget.

Be happy—
If you're humble and do not brag
You'll own the earth, not just a rag.

Be happy—
If you seek what's good and true
I shall give truth unto you.

Be happy—
If you're kind and quick to forgive
You'll have mercy as long as you live.

Be happy—
If your heart is honest and pure,
You shall see God—and that's for sure.

Be happy—
If you're peaceful and do not fight,
You'll be a child of God alright.

Be happy—
If people make fun of you because
You follow Me and are My friends.

Be happy—
If people lie or hurt you bad,
Then sweet blessings I will send.

Rejoice! Be happy! Be glad, not sad!

Jesus taught about many more things,
Especially the joy
    God's forgiveness brings.

The silly young scribes didn't write a word.
They thought that Jesus was quite absurd.

"Be happy," they laughed, "being pure and meek!
Around this place you wouldn't last a week."

It was poor old Basil who spoke up first.
"I'm happy! God loves me at my worst."

The widow smiled, "I'm not alone.
I'm grateful for the mercy God has shown."

The two fussy men hugged one another
And went away happy like brother to brother.

The Roman soldier shook his head,
For he'd been touched by what'd been said.

Old Simon, the scribe who had given his best,
Had heard the Messiah; he knew he'd been blessed!

Anna felt better; she wasn't sad.
Jesse did too; he wasn't mad.

"Jesus said we all are blessed
With joy and hope and righteousness.

"When our days go, oh so wrong,
We'll remember these words,
        and we'll be strong:

"Rejoice! Be happy! Be glad, not sad!
God loves you,
        even when you've been bad."

Dear Parent

Little children often feel sad and very frustrated with their school work, homelife, and play. Anna and Jesse felt this way. Everything and everybody around them looked very bad and hopeless. People were shouting at each other, the sick and the weak were everywhere, and no one looked happy.

From amidst all of the problems that face children today comes the shout, "To the mountain we must go! The Son of God is here, Jesus of Nazareth." Jesus stands and the crowd becomes quiet. Everyone listens to His words.

Jesus' Beatitudes declare what He is, and what He gives freely to all Christians who hear His words. On that mountain the Holy Spirit worked through Jesus' words and changed sorrow into joy, and despair into hope for all who heard and believed. Jesse and Anna's faith in Jesus as their Lord and Savior was strengthened. Paul tells us in Romans 10:17, "So faith comes from what is heard, and what is heard comes by the preaching of Christ." And the author of Proverbs 16:20 adds, "Happy is he who trusts in the Lord."

Discuss with your children why Jesse and Anna's sadness is turned to joy—hearing the Word of God. As forgiven children they can be happy and say like the twins of our story, "Be happy! Be glad! God loves you for Jesus' sake."

The Editor